HOW TO MAKE MONEY ONLINE

A Practical Guide

kouadio konan joel

I

CONTENTS

HOW TO MAKE MONEY ONLINE

A Practical Guide

PREFACE

Dear reader,

Welcome to this book entitled "How to Make Money Online". In an ever-changing world, the opportunities to earn money have undergone a major revolution with the advent of the Internet. Today, the potential for making money online is immense, giving everyone the opportunity to turn their skills, passions and ideas into sustainable sources of income.

This book was designed to accompany you on your journey to online success. Whether you are a budding entrepreneur, content creator, artist, student or professional looking for new opportunities, you will discover in these pages practical advice, proven strategies and inspiring ideas to monetize your talents and knowledge. on the Web.

As the chapters progress, we will together explore the changing online business landscape, analyzing the benefits and skills needed to succeed in this field. We'll dive into the basics of online monetization, from classic methods like affiliate marketing and product selling, to emerging trends like Nfts and the online gig economy.

You will also discover the importance of perseverance and evolution to succeed in this constantly changing universe. By remaining adaptable, continually learning, and being tenacious, you will be able to overcome challenges and thrive on your journey to online success.

It's time to seize the opportunities offered by the digital world, but it also requires strategic thinking and a balanced approach. this book will guide you step by step through discovering your niche, creating quality content, choosing the right online platforms, implementing effective marketing strategies and much more.

I invite you to dive into these pages with enthusiasm and curiosity. Each chapter will provide you with valuable knowledge and tools to grow your online presence and turn your aspirations into a successful reality.

May this book inspire you, motivate you and push you to take action. Always remember that the key to online success lies in your determination to create, innovate and adapt to the opportunities that come your way.

I wish you a rewarding journey through the exciting world of making money online.

CHAPTER 1: INTRODUCTION

Welcome to this handy guide on how to make money online. Over the past few decades, the economic landscape has undergone significant change thanks to the advent of the Internet and digital technologies. These advancements have opened new doors and offered unprecedented opportunities for generating income online.

1.1.1 The expansion of the Internet

In the 1990s, the Internet became accessible to the general public, paving the way for rapid and global communication and information exchange. Businesses quickly realized the potential of this new platform and started exploring ways to monetize it.

1.1.2 The emergence of e-commerce

One of the first areas to benefit from the Internet was e-commerce. Businesses have started creating online stores, allowing consumers to purchase products and services directly from their homes. This new form of commerce has eliminated geographical constraints and opened up a global market for online entrepreneurs.

1.1.3 The rise of online marketing

With the expansion of the Internet, online marketing has become a powerful tool for businesses. Digital marketing channels such as search engines, social media and email have provided opportunities for precise targeting, allowing companies to reach specific audiences and measure the effectiveness of their advertising campaigns.

1.1.4 The sharing economy and the platform economy

Another major development has been the emergence of the sharing economy and online platforms. Businesses have created marketplaces where individuals can offer their goods, skills or services to other users via online platforms. This has opened up new opportunities for people wishing to earn money using their existing resources.

1.1.5 The democratization of content creation

With the rise of social media platforms and content sharing platforms, content creation has become a viable avenue for generating income online. Bloggers, YouTubers, podcasters, and influencers have been able to grow a loyal following and monetize their content through advertising, brand partnerships, fan donations, and product or service sales.

1.1.6 The remote work revolution

The advent of high-speed Internet and online communication tools has also enabled the rise of remote working. Freelancers, entrepreneurs and employees can now work from anywhere in the world, collaborate remotely and offer their services to clients located all over the world.

In conclusion, the changing economic landscape, propelled by the internet and digital technologies, has created fertile ground for making money online. This development has opened up unprecedented opportunities for entrepreneurs, content creators, service providers and freelancers, allowing them to find sources of income and achieve their professional aspirations in the ever-changing digital world.

1.2 The benefits of making money online

Earning money online has many advantages that make it an attractive option for many people.

Here are some of the main benefits:

1.2.1 Flexibility and freedom

One of the most obvious benefits of making money online is the flexibility it offers. You can work at your own pace, choose your own hours and decide where you want to work. You are not limited by a fixed workplace and you have the freedom to create your own schedule according to your needs and preferences. This can be particularly advantageous for people who are looking for a balance between their professional and personal life, or for those who prefer to work independently.

1.2.2 Unlimited earning potential

When it comes to making money online, there's usually no upper limit to what you can earn. Unlike many traditional jobs where your earnings are often capped by a fixed salary, online your earnings are often tied to your work, your skills, and your ability to seize the right opportunities. You have the opportunity to increase your income by investing more time, effort and resources in your online business.

1.2.3 Reduced costs and rapid start-up

Launching an online business or starting an online business often requires much lower costs compared to setting up a physical business. You don't need to rent commercial space, invest in large inventory, or hire a large team. Many online businesses can be started with minimal budget and you can start generating income quickly. This makes online entrepreneurship more accessible and less risky for many people.

1.2.4 Access to a wide audience

The Internet gives you access to a global audience. You are not limited to a specific geographical area. You can reach people all over the world and reach a much larger audience than would be possible with a physical business. This opens up significant growth and revenue generation opportunities as you can reach potential customers in different countries and continents.

1.2.5 Various revenue opportunities

When you make money online, you have access to a multitude of different income opportunities. Whether through affiliate marketing, selling products or services online, content creation, coaching, online courses, mobile apps, freelancing services, online investments, there are a wide variety of methods to generate income online. This allows you to choose the method that best suits your interests, skills, and goals.

In conclusion, making money online offers significant benefits, such as flexibility, unlimited earning potential, lower costs, access to a large audience, and diversity of earning opportunities. It is an attractive option for those who wish to take control of their career, work independently and exploit the opportunities offered by the digital world.

1.3 Necessary skills

To be successful in making money online, it is important to develop certain key skills. Although the skills required may vary depending on the method chosen, here are some essential skills:

1.3.1 Communication skills

Effective communication is crucial when working online. Whether you choose affiliate marketing, content creation, online services, or any other method, you need to be able to communicate clearly and engagingly with your target audience. It involves the ability to write persuasively, present ideas convincingly, and respond to the questions and concerns of people you interact with online.

1.3.2 Technical skills

Some online methods may require basic technical skills. For example, if you plan to create a website or start an e-commerce, it can be useful to learn the basics of programming, SEO (Search Engine Optimization) or website management. Even if you don't plan to become a technical expert, having a basic understanding of these concepts can help you better navigate the online world.

1.3.3 Marketing skills

Understanding the basics of online marketing is key to promoting your products, services, or content. This includes knowledge of digital marketing strategies, such as SEO, social media, online advertising, and email marketing. You must be able to create an effective marketing strategy and optimize your efforts to reach your target audience effectively.

1.3.4 Time management and organizational skills

Working online requires good time management

and organizational skills. You are responsible for your schedule and must be able to prioritize tasks, meet deadlines and maintain high productivity. The ability to plan, track your progress, and stay organized is essential to successful online moneymaking.

1.3.5 Problem-solving and lifelong learning skills

One of the important aspects of making money online is the ability to problem solve and adapt to change. The digital world is changing rapidly, and it is crucial to stay up to date with new trends, new technologies and new strategies. You must be ready to learn continuously, adapt to changes and find creative solutions to problems that arise.

In conclusion, to be successful in making money online, it is important to develop communication skills, basic technical skills, marketing skills, time management skills, and problem solving skills. Continuous learning and adaptability are also essential skills to thrive in the ever-changing landscape of the online economy.

CHAPTER 2: THE BASICS OF ONLINE MONETIZATION

2.1 Identify your niche

When looking to make money online, identifying your niche is essential. Your niche is a specific segment of the market in which you will specialize. This allows you to focus on a particular target audience and build expertise in that area.

Here are some steps to identify your niche:

2.1.1 Analyze your interests and skills

Start by assessing your personal interests and the areas in which you have specific skills or knowledge. It's best to choose a niche that you are passionate about, as this will motivate you to stay engaged and provide quality content. Think about your hobbies, work experiences, and unique skills.

2.1.2 Research the market

Once you've identified a few potential areas of interest, do some in-depth market research. Analyze the demand in each niche, identify the specific needs and problems your target audience faces, and assess the existing competition. Keyword research tools and social media platforms can be helpful in understanding trends and conversations in each niche.

2.1.3 Define your
target audience

Based on your research, clearly define your target audience. Who are the people you want to reach and help with your content or products? Identify their demographics, interests, needs and challenges. The more you understand your target audience, the better you can tailor your offer to their expectations.

2.1.4 Assess the potential
for profitability

Once you've identified a specific niche and target audience, assess the potential for profitability. Examine the revenue opportunities in this niche, whether through products, services, advertising, or other monetization methods. Also consider long-term growth trends and prospects to ensure your niche has sustainable potential.

2.1.5 Refine your positioning

To stand out in your niche, you need to refine your positioning. Identify what makes you unique and different from other market players. What is your value proposition? What sets your content or products apart from others available? Find a unique angle or distinctive approach to position yourself as an expert and engage your target audience.

2.1.6 Test and adjust

Once you have chosen your niche, it is important to test your ideas and collect feedback. Post content, offer products or services on a small scale, and see how your audience responds. Learn from your results, adjust your strategy as needed, and continue to adapt based on the changing needs of your audience.

In conclusion, identifying your niche is a crucial step in successfully making money online. By combining your interests, skills and the needs of your target audience, you can create a unique and relevant offer. Be prepared to refine your positioning as you gain experience and better understand your niche's expectations.

2.2 Create quality content

When looking to make money online, creating quality content is key to attracting and retaining your audience. Whether you choose to write blog posts, create videos, produce podcasts, or develop social media content, here are some tips for creating quality content:

2.2.1 Understand your target audience

To create quality content, you need to have a deep understanding of your target audience. Identify their needs, interests, challenges and concerns. What are the problems they face and how can you help them solve them? By having a deep understanding of your target audience, you can create relevant and useful content.

2.2.2 Provide added value

Quality content should offer added value to your audience. Contribute relevant information, practical advice, innovative ideas or unique perspectives. Your content should answer your audience's questions, inspire, inform or entertain them in a way that keeps them coming back for more.

2.2.3 Be authentic

The key to creating engaging content is to be authentic. Express yourself with your own voice and share your expertise or personal experiences. Authenticity creates a connection with your audience and encourages them to engage more with your content.

2.2.4 Be creative

Creativity is an important part of standing out in a saturated online landscape. Find unique ways to showcase your content and capture your audience's attention. Use creative formats such as infographics, animated videos, themed podcasts, interactive tutorials, etc.

2.2.5 Opt for visual quality

The visual quality of your content is also crucial. Use attractive images, well-produced videos and a neat layout. Make sure your content is easy to read and pleasing to the eye by using legible fonts, harmonious colors, and a clear layout.

2.2.6 Be consistent

Consistency is key to building a loyal following. Post content regularly to keep your audience engaged. Develop an editorial calendar and stick to it. By being consistent in creating and posting content, you will build trust with your audience.

2.2.7 Interact with your audience

Engaging with your audience is key to creating great content. Respond to comments, questions, and messages from your audience. Engage in conversations and consider feedback and suggestions from your audience. It shows that you care about your audience and are ready to support them.

2.2.8 Analyze the results

Monitor the performance of your content by analyzing statistics and feedback

. Identify the types of content that work best, the topics that get the most engagement, and the formats that generate the most interest. Use this information to refine your content strategy and provide an ever better experience for your audience.

In conclusion, creating quality content is a key part of making money online. By understanding your target audience, providing added value, being authentic and creative, you can attract and retain your audience. Consistency and interaction with your audience is also key to building a strong relationship. Pay attention to the results and adapt your strategy accordingly to continue to provide quality content.

2.3 Choose the right online platforms

When you want to make money online, choosing the right platforms to deliver your content, promote your products or services, and engage with your audience is essential. Here are some tips to help you choose the right online platforms:

2.3.1 Define your goals

Before choosing a platform, clearly define your goals. What do you want to accomplish online? Do you want to sell physical or digital products? Do you want to share your expertise through content? Do you need a platform to interact with your audience? By having a clear vision of your objectives, you will be able to better choose the platforms that correspond to your needs.

2.3.2 Know your target audience

Knowing your target audience is key to choosing the right online platforms. Identify online channels where your target audience is active and engaged2.3.3 Research platforms relevant to your niche

Each niche has its own specific online platforms. Do some research to identify platforms that are popular in your area of expertise. Be sure to choose platforms that are aligned with your niche and allow you to reach your target audience.

2.3.4 Assess usability and usability

When choosing an online platform, make sure it is easy to use and user-friendly. You want to avoid complex platforms that take a long time to master. Choose platforms with an intuitive interface, functionalities adapted to your needs, and effective management tools to manage your content or your sales.

2.3.5 Consider costs and fees

Some online platforms are free, while others charge a fee for certain additional features or services. Weigh the costs and benefits of each platform you are considering. Consider listing fees, sales commissions, transaction fees, etc. Make sure the costs associated with the platform match the value it can bring to you.

2.3.6 Assess reach and visibility

The reach and visibility offered by a platform are also important. Choose platforms that allow you to reach a large audience and have a good reputation in your field. Look at traffic statistics, number of active users and engagement on the platform. Make sure that your content or products will have adequate visibility with your target audience.

2.3.7 Be flexible and adapt

The online landscape is changing rapidly, and user trends and preferences can change. Be prepared to be flexible and adapt to new platforms and changes in your audience's habits. Continue to monitor new online opportunities and feel free to adjust your strategy accordingly.

In conclusion, choosing the right online platforms is essential to making money online. Define your goals, know your target audience, research relevant platforms for your niche, assess ease of use, costs and fees, consider reach and visibility, and be prepared to be flexible. By choosing the right platforms, you can maximize your visibility, engagement, and revenue opportunities online.

2.4 Using Affiliate Marketing

Affiliate marketing is a popular strategy for making money online by recommending products or services and earning a commission on sales made through your recommendations. Here are some tips for using affiliate marketing effectively:

2.4.1 Choose relevant affiliate programs

Look for relevant affiliate programs in your niche or in areas that interest your target audience. Affiliate programs can be offered by individual companies, affiliate networks or specialized platforms. Select programs that offer quality products or services, with attractive commissions and clear terms of service.

2.4.2 Promote products you know and love

To be credible as an affiliate, it's important to promote products or services that you actually know and love. Try to test products or investigate their quality before recommending them to your audience. Your recommendation will have more impact if you can share real positive experiences or results.

2.4.3 Create engaging and persuasive content

Use your online platform (blog, website, YouTube channel, social media, etc.) to create engaging and persuasive content around the products you promote. Write detailed reviews, tutorials, comparisons, or share testimonials and product results. Use images, videos, and testimonials to reinforce your points and engage your audience.

2.4.4 Integrate your affiliate links in a natural way

Integrate your affiliate links naturally into your content, without being too promotional. Avoid aggressive messages or excessive advertisements that could turn off your audience. Include links contextually, accompanying them with a clear explanation of the product's benefits and how it can help your audience.

2.4.5 Be transparent with your audience

Transparency is essential in affiliate marketing. Let your audience know that you use affiliate links and that you receive a commission on sales. This builds trust and integrity in your relationship with your audience. Avoid deceptive practices or product endorsements that you don't actually support.

2.4.6 Track your performance

and optimize your campaigns

Use analytics tools and reports provided by affiliate programs to track your performance. Identify the products that generate the most sales and the strategies that work best. Based on this information, optimize your affiliate campaigns by adjusting your content, testing new approaches and identifying new opportunities.

2.4.7 Maintain a relationship of trust with your audience

Maintaining a relationship of trust with your audience is essential for success in affiliate marketing.

Respond to your audience's questions and concerns, offer ongoing support, and ensure that you promote only quality products. By building a relationship of trust, you will encourage your audience to follow your recommendations and make purchases through your affiliate links.

In conclusion, affiliate marketing can be an effective strategy for making money online. Choose relevant affiliate programs, promote products you know and love, create engaging and persuasive content, integrate your affiliate links naturally, be transparent with your audience, track your performance and maintain a relationship of trust with your audience. By combining these tips, you can optimize your affiliate marketing efforts and increase your online income.

2.5 Offer products or services

If you want to make money online, another approach is to offer your own products or services. Here are some tips to help you succeed in this process:

2.5.1 Identify your area of expertise

Start by identifying your area of expertise or your particular skills. What do you master? What are your passions and interests? By identifying your area of expertise, you will be able to develop products or services that match your knowledge and skills.

2.5.2 Assess market demand

Once you have identified your area of expertise, assess the market demand for products or services related to that area. Do some research to understand if your idea is sought after by consumers online. You can use keyword research tools, consult online forums or groups, or even conduct surveys with your target audience to gain valuable insights.

2.5.3 Create a quality
product or service

When developing your own product or service, be sure to deliver exceptional quality. Whether it's an e-book, online course, software, or consulting service, your offering must be of value to your audience. Spend time and effort researching, planning, and developing your product or service to ensure it meets the needs and expectations of your potential customers.

2.5.4 Use online platforms to
sell your products or services

There are many online platforms where you can sell your products or services. You can create your own website and integrate a payment system or even use online training platforms if you offer courses. Choose the platform that best suits your needs and business model.

2.5.5 Establish your
online presence

To attract customers and promote your products or services, you need to establish your online presence. Create a professional website where you can present your offer and provide relevant information to your audience. Use social networks to share content, interact with your audience and promote your products or services. Also use SEO techniques to improve your visibility in search engines.

2.5.6 Provide excellent customer service

Customer service is crucial to building a strong online reputation. Make sure you respond quickly to questions and requests from your customers. Be friendly, professional and deal with any issues efficiently. By providing excellent customer service, you will be able to retain existing customers and attract new customers through positive word-of-mouth.

2.5.7 Promote your products or services

To attract customers, it is important to promote your products or services. Use online marketing techniques such as content marketing, email marketing, paid advertising, or partnering with other online influencers or entrepreneurs. Also use SEO strategies to improve your website's visibility in search engines.

In conclusion, offering your own products or services is another way to make money online. Identify your area of expertise, gauge market demand, create a quality product or service, use online platforms to sell, establish your online presence, provide excellent customer service, and promote your products or services. By using these tips, you can build a profitable and successful online business.

2.6 Online advertising

Online advertising is another effective strategy for making money online. It allows you to promote products, services or content to a large targeted audience. Here are some tips for using online advertising effectively:

2.6.1 Define your advertising objectives

Before starting any online advertising campaign, clearly define your goals. Do you want to generate direct sales, increase your visibility, drive traffic to your website, or promote a specific offer? By having clear goals, you will be able to design ads and measure their effectiveness appropriately.

2.6.2 Identify your target audience

Knowing your target audience is key to creating effective ads. Determine the demographics, interests and behaviors of your target audience. Use online advertising targeting tools to reach precisely the people who are likely to be interested in your offer.

2.6.3 Choose the right advertising platforms

There are many online advertising platforms, such as Google Ads, Facebook Ads, Instagram Ads, Twitter Ads and many more. Select the platforms that best match your target audience and advertising goals. Each platform has its own unique features and targeting options, so be sure to do your research thoroughly to choose the ones that best suit your needs.

2.6.4 Create engaging and compelling ads

When creating your online advertisements, make sure they are attractive and compelling. Use high-quality images or videos, compelling titles, and clear descriptions. Highlight the benefits and unique features of your offer. Test different ad variations to see which perform best.

2.6.5 Optimize your advertising campaigns

Once your ads are launched, carefully monitor their performance and optimize them based on the results. Analyze key metrics such as click-through rate, conversion rate, and ROI. Identify the best performing ads and adjust your budget, targeting or content accordingly to maximize results.

2.6.6 Use monitoring and measurement tools

Use tracking and measurement tools like Google Analytics to track the effectiveness of your advertising campaigns. These tools let you know how many people clicked on your ads, how many made purchases or filled out a contact form, and other important data to gauge the success of your campaigns.

2.6.7 Be prepared to adjust your strategy

Online advertising is changing rapidly, so it's important to be prepared to adjust your strategy based on results and market trends. Experiment with different ad formats, platforms, and messages. Learn from your previous campaigns and adapt accordingly to maximize your chances of success.

In conclusion, online advertising can be an effective way to make money online. Define your goals, identify your target audience, choose the right advertising platforms, create engaging ads, optimize your campaigns, use tracking and measurement tools, and be ready to adjust your strategy. With a thoughtful approach and careful monitoring, online advertising can help you increase your visibility, attract new customers and increase your online revenue.

2.7 Crowdfunding

Crowdfunding, also known as crowdfunding, is an online fundraising method where a large number of people contribute financially to a project or business. Here are some tips for using crowdfunding effectively:

2.7.1 Clearly define your project

Before launching a crowdfunding campaign, clearly define your project. What is your fundraising goal? What are the objectives and benefits for contributors? Be sure to present your project in a clear, compelling, and engaging way to pique the interest of potential contributors.

2.7.2 Choose the appropriate crowdfunding platform

There are many crowdfunding platforms online, such as Kickstarter, Indiegogo, GoFundMe, and many more. Each platform has its own characteristics and rules, so choose the one that best suits your project. Research the available platforms, review the fees and terms, and choose the one that offers the features and audience best suited to your project.

2.7.3 Create an attractive crowdfunding campaign

The key to a successful crowdfunding campaign is to create an attractive and compelling page for your project. Use images, videos, and detailed descriptions to showcase your project in an engaging way. Clearly explain the purpose of your fundraiser, how the funds will be used, and the benefits contributors will receive in return.

2.7.4 Set contribution levels and rewards

To encourage contributions, set contribution levels with corresponding rewards. Offer attractive incentives to encourage contributors to give more. Rewards can be products, exclusive services, special thanks, honorable mentions , or anything else that fits your project.

2.7.5 Promote your crowdfunding campaign

Promotion is essential to attract contributors to your crowdfunding campaign. Use social networks, your website, your personal and professional network to publicize your project and encourage people to contribute. Share regular updates on your campaign's progress and publicly thank contributors.

2.7.6 Communicate and maintain a relationship with contributors

When you receive contributions, communicate regularly with your contributors to keep them informed of the progress of your project. Answer their questions, provide updates, and express your gratitude for their support. Transparent communication and a strong relationship with your contributors can help you retain your support base and encourage additional contributions.

2.7.7 Respect your commitments to contributors

When your crowdfunding campaign is successful and you receive the necessary funds, be sure to honor your commitments to contributors. Deliver the promised rewards in a timely manner and keep them informed of any important developments. This will help maintain contributor trust and satisfaction.

In conclusion, crowdfunding can be an effective way to raise funds online for your project or business. Clearly define your project, choose the right crowdfunding platform, create an attractive campaign, set contribution levels and rewards, promote your campaign, communicate with your contributors and meet your commitments. With careful planning and solid execution, crowdfunding can help you secure the financial resources needed to make your online ventures a reality.

2.8 Brand partnerships and sponsorships

Brand partnerships and sponsorships are effective strategies for making money online by collaborating with other businesses or influencers. Here are some tips for taking advantage of these opportunities:

2.8.1 Identify suitable brand partners

The first step is to identify brand partners who are complementary to your field of activity and your target audience. Look for businesses or people who share similar values and have a similar audience to yours. It is important to choose partners who can add value to your project and to your potential customers.

2.8.2 Establish a clear value proposition

Before contacting potential partners, establish a

clear value proposition. Explain how collaborating with you can benefit both your partner and your shared audience. Highlight mutual benefits, such as growing audiences, sharing resources, increasing sales, or creating joint content.

2.8.3 Approach potential partners professionally

Once you've identified potential partners, approach them professionally. Introduce yourself and explain why you think a collaboration could be beneficial for both parties. Be clear and precise in your communications and highlight what you can offer in terms of added value and expected results.

2.8.4 Establish strong partnership agreements

When entering into brand partnerships or sponsorships, establishing solid agreements is essential. Clearly define the roles and responsibilities of each party, common goals, expectations and financial terms. Make sure that agreements are mutually beneficial and that they are put in writing to avoid misunderstandings later.

2.8.5 Collaborate actively with your partners

Once the partnership is established, actively

collaborate with your partners. Create joint content, organize online events, share cross-ads or special promotions. The key is to engage your common audience and build trust and interest in your products or services.

2.8.6 Monitor results and adjust strategy if necessary

Carefully monitor the results of your brand partnerships and sponsorships. Analyze data, sales, interactions and feedback from your audience. If certain strategies are not yielding the expected results, feel free to adjust your approach or explore new partnership opportunities.

2.8.7 Cultivate long-term relationships

To succeed in brand partnerships and sponsorships, it is essential to nurture long-term relationships with your partners. Stay in regular contact, share success stories, collaborate on new projects, and keep looking for ways to mutually improve your online business.

In conclusion, brand partnerships and sponsorships can be lucrative strategies for making money online. Identify suitable brand partners, establish a clear value proposition, approach them professionally, establish strong agreements, collaborate actively, monitor results and nurture long-term relationships. With a strategic approach and successful collaboration, brand partnerships and sponsorships can help increase your online visibility, credibility and revenue.

CHAPTER 3: AFFILIATE MARKETING

3.1 What is affiliate marketing?

Affiliate marketing is an online marketing model in which a person (the affiliate) promotes the products or services of another company (the advertiser) and receives a commission from the sales made through their efforts. promotion. It is a form of performance-based marketing, where the affiliate is paid only when concrete results are obtained, such as sales, registrations or clicks.

Affiliate marketing works through unique affiliate links assigned to each affiliate. When a visitor clicks on the affiliate link and performs a predefined action, such as a purchase, the affiliate is credited with that sale and receives a commission on the amount of the sale.

Affiliate programs are often run by affiliate networks or directly by advertisers. Affiliates can choose from a wide range of products or services to promote, depending on their niche, audience, and interests.

Affiliate marketing has many benefits for affiliates. It allows you to make money online without having to create or manage a product, store goods or deal with customer service. Plus, it offers the flexibility to work from anywhere, anytime, based on your own availability.

For advertisers, affiliate marketing is a profitable strategy because they only pay when results are achieved. They can also benefit from the expertise and audience of affiliates to promote their products or services to a wider audience.

In summary, affiliate marketing is an online marketing model where the affiliate promotes the products or services of another company and is paid according to the results obtained. It is a popular and profitable method of making money online by exploiting the audience and credibility of other businesses.

3.2 How marketing

works affiliate ?

Affiliate marketing works on the basis of a partnership between the affiliate and the advertiser. Here are the main steps in the process:

1. The affiliate signs up for an affiliate program offered by the advertiser. These programs are often available on advertisers' websites or affiliate platforms.

2. Once registered, the affiliate receives a unique affiliate link that allows them to track sales or actions made by referred visitors from their website, blog, social media page or other promotional channel.

3. Affiliate promotes advertiser's products or services using their affiliate link. This may include reviews, recommendations, reviews, articles, videos, advertisements or other forms of content.

4. When a visitor clicks on the affiliate's affiliate link and performs a specific action, such as a purchase or signup, the affiliate is credited with the sale and receives a predefined commission.

5. Advertiser manages the sales process, including product delivery, customer service, and tracking of sales assigned to each Affiliate.

6. Affiliate receives regular payments based on sales made through their promotional efforts.

3.3 The Benefits of Affiliate Marketing

Affiliate marketing offers many benefits for affiliates who want to make money online. Here are some of those benefits:

3.3.1 No need to create a product or service

One of the main benefits of affiliate marketing is that it allows you to promote existing products or services, without having to create them yourself. This saves you the time and resources needed to design, develop and bring a product to market.

3.3.2 No stock management or customer service

As an affiliate, you don't have to worry about product inventory management or customer service. The advertiser takes care of these aspects, allowing you to focus on promoting and generating sales.

3.3.3 Passive income potential

Once you have your promotion system in place and driving traffic to your affiliate links, you can generate passive income. Sales can keep happening even when you're not actively working, allowing you to earn money even while you sleep.

3.3.4 Wide choice of products or services

Affiliate marketing gives you access to a huge range of products or services to promote. You can choose products or services that match your niche, interests, or audience, increasing your chances of generating sales.

3.3.5 Flexibility and freedom

As an affiliate, you have the freedom to choose when and where you want to promote the advertiser's products or services. You can work at your own pace, from anywhere, as long as you have an internet connection.

3.4 How to Succeed in Affiliate Marketing

To succeed in affiliate marketing, here are some important tips to follow:

3.4.1 Choose Quality Products or Services Be sure to promote quality products or services as this builds your credibility and increases the chances that visitors will make a purchase after clicking on your affiliate link.

3.4.2 Target your audience: Identify your target audience and focus your promotional efforts on them. The more your audience is relevant and interested in the products or services you promote, the more you increase your chances of generating sales.

3.4.3 Create quality content: Produce engaging and informative content that engages your audience and demonstrates the value of the products or services you are promoting. Use different forms of content, such as blog posts, videos, reviews, tutorials, to attract and convince your audience.

3.4.4 Be transparent and honest: Be transparent and honest with your audience about your affiliate status. Make it clear that you receive a commission on sales made through your affiliate links. This builds trust with your audience and maintains your credibility.

3.4.5 Experiment and optimize: Test different promotion strategies, track results, and optimize your approach based on data and feedback. This iterative process will allow you to continually improve your performance and income as an affiliate.

In conclusion, affiliate marketing is an effective way to make money online by promoting the products or services of other businesses. By choosing the right products, targeting your audience, creating quality content, and being transparent, you can succeed as an affiliate and generate passive income from your promotional efforts. Affiliate marketing offers the flexibility and freedom to work at your own pace, while leveraging the expertise and audience of other businesses to increase your online income.

CHAPTER 4: CONTENT CREATION

Content creation refers to the process of producing and distributing various types of content online, such as blog posts, videos, podcasts, images, infographics, e-books, guides, posts on social networks, etc. The main objective of content creation is to provide added value to a specific target audience.

4.1 The importance of quality content

In the online world, content is king. Creating quality content is a key part of being successful in online monetization. Whether through a blog, videos, podcasts or social media posts, content plays a vital role in attracting and engaging your audience. Here are a few reasons why quality content is so important:

4.1.1 Value for your audience: Quality content provides real value to your audience. It answers their questions, solves their problems, informs them, entertains them or inspires them. When your audience finds your content useful and relevant, they're more likely to stay loyal and come back for more content in the future.

4.1.2 Credibility and expertise Creating quality content demonstrates your credibility and expertise in your field of activity. This builds your audience's trust in you as an expert, which can positively influence their decision to buy or engage with the products or services you recommend.

4.1.3 Engagement and sharing: Quality content engages your audience. When your content is interesting, informative, entertaining, or emotionally engaging, it encourages comments, shares, and interactions with your audience. This helps increase your reach and visibility online, which can lead to growth in your audience and monetization potential.

4.1.4 Search Engine Optimization: Quality content is also important for SEO. Search engines, such as Google, are placing increasing importance on content quality when determining rankings in search results. Well-written, informative, and relevant content is more likely to appear at the top of search results, increasing your website's visibility and your ability to attract organic traffic.

4.2 Types of content

There are several types of content you can create to grow your online presence and generate income. Here are some examples :

4.2.1 Blog posts: Blog posts are one of the most popular types of content. They allow you to dive deeper into topics, share tips, tutorials, case studies or analysis. Blog posts are great for SEO, social media sharing, and building a loyal following.

4.2.2 Videos: Videos are increasingly popular and offer a wide variety of formats, such as tutorials, vlogs, presentations, interviews, etc. Platforms like YouTube and TikTok offer opportunities for monetization through advertising, brand partnerships, and affiliations.

4.2.3 Podcasts: Podcasts are audio files that listeners can stream or download. They offer a convenient way to share information, discussions and interviews. Podcasts can be monetized through advertising, brand partnerships, and listener donations.

4.2.4 Social Media: Posting on social media, such as Facebook, Instagram, Twitter and LinkedIn, is a great way to share short, engaging content with your audience. You can use these platforms to promote longer content, direct traffic to your website or other monetization channels.

4.2.5 e-Books and Guides: Creating e-books and guides helps bring your expertise together in a longer, structured format. You can sell them directly on your website or use them as an incentive to sign up for your email list.

4.3 Content creation strategies

To create quality content, here are some strategies to consider:

4.3.1 Know your audience: Understand your audience's needs, interests and preferences. This will allow you to create relevant content that is adapted to their expectations.

4.3.2 Provide value: Make sure your content provides real value to your audience. Answer their questions, solve their problems and share useful information.

4.3.3 Look after the presentation: Write content that is well structured, easy to read and visually appealing. Use headings, subheadings, bulleted lists, and images to make it easier to understand and read.

4.3.4 Be Regular and Consistent: Post content regularly to keep your audience engaged. Create an editorial calendar and stick to it as much as possible.

4.3.5 Use keywords: Conduct relevant keyword research for your content to optimize SEO and attract organic traffic.

4.3.6 Encourage interaction: Encourage your audience to comment, share and interact with your content. Respond to comments and create a sense of community around your content.

In summary, creating quality content is essential for success in online monetization. Valuable content, tailored to your audience, can boost your credibility, increase your visibility, boost engagement and boost SEO. Explore different types of content and use effective strategies to create engaging and relevant content for your audience.

CHAPTER 5: ELECTRONIC COMMERCE

5.1 What is e-commerce?

E-commerce, also known as online commerce, refers to the buying and selling of goods and services through the Internet. It is a form of commercial transaction that allows consumers to make purchases online from online sellers or shops.

E-commerce encompasses a wide range of activities, ranging from purchases of physical products, such as clothing, electronics or household items, to online services, such as hotel reservations, airline tickets or subscriptions to streaming platforms. Transactions can be made using a computer, smartphone, tablet or other internet-connected devices.

5.2 The benefits of e-commerce

E-commerce has many benefits for consumers and sellers. Here are some of the main benefits of e-commerce:

5.2.1 Accessibility and Convenience: E-commerce allows consumers to purchase products or services anytime and from anywhere without having to physically travel to a store. This provides great convenience and flexibility, which is especially beneficial for busy people or people who don't have easy access to physical stores.

5.2.2 Wide choice of products: Online stores offer a wide range of products from different brands, different countries and different categories. Consumers have access to a greater selection of products, allowing them to compare prices, features and customer reviews before making a purchase.

5.2.3 Cost Savings: E-commerce can save consumers money by avoiding travel costs, parking costs, food costs and other expenses associated with in-store purchases. Online sellers can also save on the costs of renting physical business premises, which can translate into more competitive prices for products.

5.2.4 Personalization and Recommendations: E-commerce platforms often use algorithms to recommend products or services based on consumer preferences and buying behaviors. This allows for a more personalized shopping experience, where consumers can discover new products that match their interests.

5.2.5 Order Tracking and Management: E-commerce provides the ability to easily track order status, receive notifications about updates, and conveniently manage product returns or exchanges. This allows consumers to have more precise control over their purchases and makes it easier to resolve any problems that may arise.

5.3 Types of e-commerce

There are different types of e-commerce, suitable for different types of products or services.

Here Are Some Common Examples:

5.3.1 B2C (Business-to-Consumer) e-commerce: This is e-commerce between businesses and consumers. Businesses sell their products or services directly to consumers through websites or online platforms.

5.3.2 B2B (Business-to-Business) electronic commerce: In this case, electronic commerce takes place between companies. Businesses buy and sell products, services or information to other businesses through online platforms or electronic trading systems.

5.3.3 C2C (Consumer-to-Consumer) e-commerce: C2C e-commerce involves direct transactions between consumers. Individuals sell products or services to other individuals through online platforms that facilitate peer-to-peer transactions.

5.3.4 C2B (Consumer-to-Business) e-commerce: In this model, consumers offer their products, services or skills to businesses. Individuals can, for example, sell their artistic creations, offer consulting services or offer product reviews.

5.4 E-commerce platforms

There are several popular e-commerce platforms that allow sellers to create and manage their online store. Some of the major platforms include:

5.4.1 Shopify: An all-in-one e-commerce platform that allows users to easily create their online store, manage products, orders, payments and access various customization and integration features .

5.4.2 WooCommerce: An e-commerce plugin for WordPress that makes it easy to transform a WordPress site into a functional online store.

5.4.3 Amazon: The world's largest e-commerce platform, which allows sellers to sell their products directly on Amazon's website and benefit from its huge customer base.

5.4.4 eBay: An e-commerce platform based on auctions and auctions, which allows sellers to offer used or new products to interested buyers.

5.4.5 Etsy : A platform focused on artisan products, handmade creations and unique items, which allows sellers to connect with a community of buyers looking for original products.

5.5 Steps to launch an online store

If you want to get started in e-commerce by creating your own online store, here are some steps to follow:

5.5.1 Define your product or service: Identify the product or service you want to sell online. Conduct market research to assess demand, competition, and opportunities.

5.5.2 Choose an e-commerce platform: Select an e-commerce platform that suits your needs and budget. Explore features, fees, ease of use, and customization options.

5.5.3 Create your online store: Set up your online store by adding products, descriptions, images, and payment and delivery information. Customize the design to reflect your brand and identity.

5.5.4 Set up payment systems: Integrate secure payment options to allow customers to pay online. Choose from common payment gateways such as

PayPal, Stripe, or credit card payment options.

5.5.5 Optimize your store for SEO: Use search engine optimization (SEO) techniques to improve the visibility of your online store in search results. Research relevant keywords, optimize tags and descriptions, and create quality content.

5.5.6 Promote your online store: Implement online marketing strategies to promote your store and attract customers. Use social media, email marketing, SEO, online advertising, partnerships, and other tactics to increase your store's visibility and drive traffic.

5.5.7 Manage Orders and Shipments: Implement effective order management, inventory tracking, and shipment management systems. Make sure you provide excellent customer service by responding quickly to questions and handling returns or issues in a professional manner.

In conclusion, e-commerce offers many opportunities for online monetization. It allows sellers to build online stores, sell products or services to a global audience, and reap the benefits of accessibility, convenience, choice, customization, and cost savings. By understanding the different e-commerce options, choosing the right platform, and implementing effective marketing strategies, it is possible to succeed in e-commerce and generate income online.

CHAPTER 6:
ONLINE SERVICES

6.1 What are online services?

Online services refer to activities and service offerings that are provided via the Internet. These services can be varied, ranging from professional services such as legal consultation or accounting, to creative services such as graphic design or copywriting, to coaching services, online courses, technical support, translation , project management , and more. Online services offer the ability to provide specific expertise or skills to a global customer base, without the geographic limitations associated with traditional services.

6.2 The advantages
of online services

Online services offer many advantages for both

providers and customers. Here are some of the main benefits:

6.2.1 Global accessibility: Online services enable providers to reach global customers. No matter where the potential clients are, it is possible to offer one's services online and work with people from different countries and cultures.

6.2.2 Working flexibility: Online services offer significant working flexibility. Providers can work remotely, choose their own hours, and set their own work pace. This allows a better balance between professional and personal life.

6.2.3 Cost Savings: Online services reduce costs associated with business premises or travel expenses. Providers can work from home or anywhere with an internet connection, reducing office rental expenses and travel costs.

6.2.4 Scalability: The online services offer great scalability. Providers can easily adjust their offering based on demand, increase or decrease their workload , and expand their service portfolio to meet changing market needs.

6.2.5 Automation of tasks: Online services make it possible to automate certain repetitive or administrative tasks, which allows service providers to save time and focus more on the essential aspects of their activity.

6.2.6 Virtual collaboration: Online services facilitate virtual collaboration with clients. Information exchanges, meetings and consultations can be carried out through online communication, video calls, emails and other remote collaboration tools.

6.3 Online service platforms

There are various online platforms that facilitate the delivery and access to online services. These platforms offer features and tools to find providers, communicate with them, manage projects and payments, and leave reviews and comments. Some of the major online service platforms include Upwork, Freelancer, Fiverr, Guru, Toptal, and many more.

6.4 How to get started with online services

If you want to offer services online, here are some steps to get started:

6.4.1 Identify your skills: Determine what your skills and expertise are. What services can you offer online? Identify your niche and what sets you apart from other providers.

6.4.2 Create your portfolio: Build an online portfolio to showcase your accomplishments, past projects and skills. This will allow potential clients to see your work and get an idea of what you can offer.

6.4.3 Join online service platforms: Register with online service platforms relevant to your field of activity. Create an engaging professional profile and enhance it with relevant information, work examples, and recommendations.

6.4.4 Network and develop your online presence: Participate in online groups and communities related to your field of activity. Make connections, share your expertise and create a strong online presence using social media, a blog or a professional website.

6.4.5 Set your rates and establish contracts: Set your rates based on your expertise, experience and the market. Develop clear contracts for each project to define expectations, deadlines, deliverables and payment terms.

6.4.6 Provide excellent customer service: Be sure to provide excellent customer service, responding quickly to customer inquiries, communicating clearly and meeting deadlines. Customer satisfaction is key to building your reputation and earning referrals.

In conclusion, online services offer many opportunities for online monetization. Whether offering professional, creative, coaching or other types of services, it is possible to provide valuable expertise to a global clientele through the Internet. By leveraging the benefits of online services, using the right platforms, and developing a strong online presence, it is possible to achieve success and generate revenue online through service delivery.

CHAPTER 7: EMERGING OPPORTUNITIES

7.1 New trends in e-commerce

The online moneymaking landscape is constantly changing, and new opportunities emerge regularly. Here are some of the emerging trends that offer exciting opportunities:

7.1.1 Dropshipping: Dropshipping is an online business model where you do not store the products you sell. Instead, you work with vendors who ship products directly to customers. This reduces costs related to storage and logistics, while offering great flexibility.

7.1.2 Print -on- Demand : Print -on- demand allows for the creation and sale of personalized products such as t-shirts, mugs, posters, etc. You can design your own patterns and print them only when you receive an order, which reduces initial costs and risks.

7.1.3 NFTs: NFTs (Non-Fungible Tokens) are unique digital assets that can represent works of art, collectibles, music tracks, etc. The NFT market is growing rapidly and provides opportunities for artists and content creators to monetize their creations.

7.1.4 E-learning: E-learning, or online learning, is growing in popularity. You can create and sell online courses on specific topics to share your expertise and help learners learn new skills.

7.1.5 Online coaching services: Online coaching in areas such as personal development, professional coaching, life coaching, etc., is increasingly in demand. If you have expertise in a specific area, you can offer online coaching services to help people achieve their goals.

7.2 Social media opportunities

Social media also offers many opportunities for online monetization. Here are some examples :

7.2.1 Influencers: If you have a strong social media presence and have developed an engaged community, you can work with brands as an influencer to promote their products or services and earn revenue through partnerships and sponsorships.

7.2.2 Social Media Affiliate Marketing: You may promote products or services using social media affiliate links. Every time someone makes a purchase through your affiliate link, you earn a commission.

7.2.3 Selling digital products: Social media can serve as a platform to sell digital products such as e-books, online courses, templates, graphic resources, etc.

7.2.4 Sponsored Content: You may be compensated for creating sponsored content on social media, where you post content highlighting specific products, services or events.

7.3 The online gig economy

With the emergence of technology and live streaming platforms, the online concert economy is growing significantly. Artists, musicians and content creators can organize paid online concerts, virtual shows, workshops and exclusive events for their audience, providing a unique experience and generating revenue through ticket sales or subscriptions .

In conclusion, it is important to stay abreast of new trends and emerging opportunities in the field of online money. The opportunities are vast and ever-changing. By exploring new trends such as dropshipping, print -on- demand , NFTs, e-learning, online coaching, social media and the online gig economy, you can find innovative ways to monetize your skills and expertise online.

CHAPTER 8: PERSEVERANCE AND EVOLUTION

8.1 The importance of online persistence

When it comes to making money online, persistence plays a crucial role in your success. Here are some reasons why persistence is important:

8.1.1 Building an Audience: It can take time to build an online audience. Perseverance will allow you to continue producing quality content, engaging with your audience, and promoting your offer, even when the results are not immediate. Over time, you can cultivate a loyal and engaged community that supports your online business.

8.1.2 Adapting to change: The online landscape is changing rapidly, with new technologies, ever-changing platform algorithms and changing user preferences. Perseverance will help you adapt to these changes, experiment with new strategies, and stay up to date with emerging trends.

8.1.3 Overcoming Obstacles: The path to online success can be littered with obstacles and challenges. There can be moments of doubt, frustration and failures. Perseverance will allow you to overcome these obstacles, stay motivated and keep moving forward despite the difficulties.

8.1.4 Continuous Learning: Making money online requires a continuous learning mindset. Best practices, effective strategies and technological tools are constantly evolving. Perseverance will encourage you to seek new knowledge, train yourself and adapt to changes in the market.

8.2 Evolution and diversification

In the online world, it is essential to remain adaptable and evolve with the needs and demands of the market. Here are some tips to promote your development and diversification:

8.2.1 Monitor trends: Stay on top of new trends, technological developments and changes in your niche. Be open to exploring new areas and new opportunities that match your skills and passion.

8.2.2 Test and Experiment: Don't be afraid to experiment with new ideas, test new business models, or offer new products or services. Testing will allow you to identify what works best for you and pivot where necessary.

8.2.3 Diversify your sources of income: Don't rely on just one source of online income. Explore different avenues to diversify your sources of income, whether through different platforms, various income models or collaborations with other professionals.

8.2.4 Learn from others: Look for mentors, experts and established professionals in your field. Learn from them, study their strategies and be inspired by their journey. Collaborating and learning from others can help you broaden your horizons and find new opportunities.

In conclusion, perseverance and evolution are essential elements for long-term success in the online world. By remaining persistent, adaptable, and open to change, you can not only grow your online income, but also continue to thrive and seize new opportunities as the online business landscape changes.

9 798857 555064